KALEIDOSCOPE

D. NANCE

D.N.

DEDICATION

For all that you are and all that you have given me.

This is for you.

From the brightest days to the darkest nights.

From the beauty within my dreams to the ugly within my

nightmares. I have created this beautiful kaleidoscope to share

with you.

CONTENTS

ACKNOWLEDGMENTS

I would like to thank everyone who supported me on this journey. I never thought I would accomplish anything like this. What started off as therapy may turn out to be one of my biggest accomplishments ever.

Special thank you to my daughter Alianna Skye for making me want to be the best me every day. I hope she looks at this as a symbol that she can do whatever she sets her mind to.

My Eyes Knew

My eyes knew I loved you before my mind could process it.
Before my heart could feel it, before your lips parted and
flowers flowed from your throat.

My eyes knew.

When they met the blue in yours.
Sky diving, no, more like free falling into an ocean.
Praying that landing doesn't shatter me into a million pieces.

Years have gone by and I still see you in my mind.
A constant reminder of how I tripped and shattered my entire
existence.

The struggle to glue all of the broken pieces back together.
A reminder of how my life would be forever changed.

When I speak to you, when I see you, I crack all over again,
but the glue holds it all together.

My eyes knew.
See my eyes knew, what my mind
and heart could not comprehend.

My eyes fell in love with every part of you.

When your lips parted and you began spitting flowers from your mouth; only then my mind understood and my heart sunk to my stomach and all that I have ever craved was you.

I loved you for how you made me feel. Wanted, appreciated, loved, like I was the most important person that you had ever laid eyes upon.

I loved you because you came into my world, you redefined the sun, the moon, and the stars.

I loved you for being you
and for accepting me.

I'm sorry that my mind could not have been as sharp as my eyes, and as strong as my heart. I have dreamt dreams of you and me.

I pray that one day I will be able to embrace you
And that one day my eyes will meet the blue in yours
and fall but just be.

Pages

I walk around like I have an "S" on my chest.

Truth

Truth is I cannot open myself like one of your books.

Damaged

I'm as weak as the glue that binds the pages together. Pages ripped, corners bent.

Regret

Regret stings as much as seeing testing results. Too many erase marks counted wrong.

Understanding

I find myself falling deeper, hoping it is only a dream. Dream turned to reality and I find myself lost in translation. Your mood, the gaze of your eyes, how do you feel?

I try

I try to understand, but please understand the pain, the experience, the failed chances, the mistakes. Those are the things that scar my heart.

Those are the things that made me who I am...the nice cover with torn and bent pages. Eraser marks!!

Think of similarities, look through the pages of your stories and relate the damaged character from the pages to the people that surround you in your everyday life.

I'll love you forever, but only if you promise to hold me and restore faith in me, cherish me as if my pages were embroidered in gold.....like God himself shot cupid and his arrow at us.

Together
Together our pages would be embroidered with hearts and everlasting faith.

Heart on My Sleeve

My gut is weaker
Than my mind.

Care
Or dare not to?

My senses remind me of
Why I love you

You feel like fresh silk sheets
Pressed upon my bare skin

Your scent is like no other;
I could get high off your fumes

Your body is your body. It does not define your beauty, but
your curves are beautiful.

You taste......You taste like I am winning even when I am
losing.

Your mind captivates me, holds me confined to one space. I
get lost in your eyes, your touch, your words. I get lost! I get
lost in you!

An hour seems like only a moment when I am wrapped up in your arms.....but

Fear rushes over me, it consumes me! My heart screams, "no more!" I can't take any more. Is she? Or is she not? Does she? Or does she not? Do I want to know? Or do I not?

Failed love has made a prisoner of my mind and an ice box of my heart.

Yet my mind fights to remind me why I love you. Your smile can be my sunrise and sunset; Just one blink of your eyes can be the wind that contains a raging fire.

Your lips bound your Prince to this form! Your touch is powerful enough to make a king.

I dreamt a dream of you and me,
And maybe one day we will be.

Soar

Does it cross your mind that my heart aches for you?

The sound of your voice is a sweet harmony that soothes my soul. Yet most days we sit in utter silence as if we are perfect strangers that have nothing to offer one another other than painful memories of our rigid past.

Promise me that you will move forward and not look back at me. You deserve so much more.

Spread your wings and soar.

As much as I have tried to move on, I think you often. Yet I cannot be with you.

There is something I find unsettling about you. It breaks my heart to think at one point I loved you so much that it hurt not to touch you. I could not get close enough to you and if your body opened up and swallowed me whole it would have been the perfect remedy.

Instead your mouth opened up and my mind swam down your throat and latched on to your heart like a leech. You were a drug that I could not get enough of. I lost myself in you. I lost my mind in us.

Promise that you will move forward and not look back at me. Someone will give you the moon and the stars.

Spread your wings and soar.

Now when it comes to you I cannot even recognize myself when I look in the mirror. I'm not blaming you for things that happened in my life, I am finished with the blame games. I just always felt you controlled me in so many ways. That's why I get an attitude, because you can't see it.

Promise that you will move forward and not look back at me. Follow your heart, be brave, spread your wings, and soar.

Poison or Prison

Once upon a time in a distant past, I craved you, I wanted you, and I dreamt of your lips pressed against mine.

Passion
My passion for you was like touching a hot stove; it burned my soul when I didn't know any better.

Sex
Sex with you was everlasting. The excitement and the joy that you gave to me was like no other. It can only be described as a dream come true.

Failure
I failed you too many times; over and over again. Two wrongs do not make it right....we failed us, but we will not fail our angel.

Freedom
We have the freedom to be trapped in prison, must we continue to poison our hearts with this pain, this neglect of respect.

Afraid

We were too afraid to see one another happy and living without each other. Why do we choose both prison and poison?

Once upon a time, in the present, we live as prisoners of war, left and forgotten by what we loved, too afraid to trust what was. Poisoned hearts and imprisoned souls!

Will you stay or let go.

Storm

I thought the storm had passed. The rumble of soldier's boots was like thunder striking open space with nothing to catch the sound.

I thought the storm had passed.
I thought the storm had passed. The screams of the sick and dying, the lost futures, was like the wind softly whispering in your ear.

I thought the storm had passed.
I thought the storm had passed. The crackling of M4s and AKs are only a reminder of the past storms and storms that are yet to come.

World

Desire nothing more then what you absolutely need,

Open your eyes and see that you have already been blessed.

Do not let our corrupt world blind you

Into thinking you have less, when you already have

everything.

Losing

Sometimes it takes losing

To make sense of all of the important things

That you have yet to gain.

One Day

The day will come when you are no longer

The first thing I crave when my eyes open.

That is the day I will know that I am over you.

Truth

Live your truth

Fear no man

Speak ill of no man

Walk with faith

Encourage

Listen

Learn

Dream

Conquer

Knowledge

He who contains knowledge for power is a fool

He who contains knowledge to share is a liberator

Self

We all lose things

We all have lost someone

We often value things we lose

More than we value ourselves

No one should be valued more than one's self

Without yourself you are nothing.

Insomnia

On nights I cannot sleep, I find myself thinking about you,
Wondering how you are doing. Wondering what you are doing.
I find myself and some of the pieces that once made me
whole.

I find myself wondering if I ever cross your mind.
Wondering why my heart aches and how I freeze up
whenever I hear your name.

I lie here and cannot help but think why God is playing a
cruel joke on me. Wondering why does he let you haunt me.
There has not been a day that you have not popped into my
head and a night that I have not dreamt about what if.

Rest of My Life

As I lay my head to rest, all I can think of is your head on my
chest. When I close my eyes, all I can do is stare into yours
Head bent back, just enough to see that smile. Just long
enough to see my life with you flash like lightning.
In that moment I knew, it was you.

It was always you.

Hold On

Hold on to me, never let me go

Dream with me; lets succeed

Walk with me through the rain

Sit with me through the pain

Time is running out, hold on to me

Wait, never let me go

I am sorry I had to go

My time, my time has gone

Hold on to me, hold me in your heart

Never let me go

Titanic

It seems like it has been forever

Then I realize I just met you.

Lets pump the brakes, take it slow

Full steam ahead we shall go, nothing can stop us

Falling like Leo and Kate

It has been about two weeks...I love you

I will never let you go

Moving too fast, clashing

Too caught up, too proud to navigate through the Icebergs

Just after three weeks, relationship sinking

I'm sorry; I have to let you go

But I thought you loved me

You said you would never let me go

You have been cold

I have to save myself from freezing

Take Me

Blast me with the flames of your desire

Drown me with your affection

Push me into your fire

Let me fall

The Build Up

Hope that you notice how I stare at you

Hope that you notice how you light up my day

Hope that my presence does the same

Hope that I get the courage to take a chance

I can only hope that your beauty does not steal my words as I

approach.

Hi, my name is Dennis.

Would you like to go out with me sometime?

Would you like to maybe see a movie?

Would you like to go for a walk and talk?

Man, I can only hope that this practice pays off.

Type of Love

I want the type of love that everyone hates
The more they hate, the more we smile type of love.

I want the type of love where communication is never an
obstacle. Just from one glance, I understand type of love.

I want the type of love that if either of us falls
We always catch each other no matter what type of love.

I want the type of love that has nothing but dreams
Together we will build an empire type of love.

I want the type of love that has its ups and downs
Through controversy we will learn and grow together type of
love.

I want the type of love that scares me every time I look into
your eyes, I get butterflies in my stomach type of love.

Every time I am away from you, it hurts not to touch you type
of love. Every time you say my name, I fall in love all over
again type of love. The type of love that loves you for you and
me for me. That Unconditional type of love.

Rumors

Created by those who find some value in your life in which
they lack in theirs.

Created by those who don't know, or think they know,

Created by those who feel threatened by your character,

Created by those who want to steal a piece of your joy,

Created by those who would rather poison and destroy,

Created by the weak minded, weak hearted, and weak
spirited.

Those who believe and speak

Without seeking their own truth

May be weaker than the one

Who started it all!

Fly be free

Release yourself from

The shackles of your mind

Peace over War

Remember to count your blessings.

Do not let your peace of mind
turn into a war zone.

Do not let the negative memories
turn into landmines.

See them for what they are
Use them for strength
To inspire instead of destroy.

Keep Moving

Sometimes you have to turn your pain into kinetic energy!

Erase

When all you can see in your mind and feel in your heart is
someone who is in the process of erasing you,
What else is there to fight for?

Teaching

Some lessons have to be learned the hard way.

It may hurt and burn you to your soul.

Understanding why you are walking through the flames is the

most important part.

Hold you

When you are gone

You will always be with me

I will hold you in my smile like the sky

Holds the sun

Breaking

Honestly we need to stop breaking our own hearts and blaming it on other people.

<u>Be More</u>

Be more than what you were yesterday

The inability to adapt within the waves of change

is a reflection of your narrow mind.

Life

Chase your dreams to the end of time

Love with every part of your soul

Believe in yourself undoubtedly

Fail and fall, learn and get back up stronger

Succeed and be humble

Open your mind to all the possibilities that this world has to

offer.

Fight battles and make peace

Live every day as if it is your last

Remember time should be valued as if it is the only thing you

can't get back.

See you

Let's just say,

Every time I close my eyes

I see you

Moon and Sun

You are the moon and I am the sun

Fate only allows us to eclipse when the time is right.

Chasing you in orbit

Waiting for our paths to realign.

Have You Ever

Have you ever looked at someone and their mere beauty took your breath away?

Have you ever craved someone so bad it hurts?

Have you ever gotten butterflies from hearing someone's name?

Have you ever felt something so deep within that no matter how hard you try to explain, words can never truly express the burning within your soul?

Love

Love as vast as the ocean...Captivating

Pulling me like the moon pulls the tide

Drown me with your laughter

Blind me with your glare

Enslave me with your siren song

Destroy

No matter how far the wind blows me
I would destroy myself over and over to find my way back to
you.

Walk Away

My heart has been ripped from my chest and lost in the darkness. I have continued to search through the dark. I bumped in to you. I know it cannot be found by someone else. All I wanted was for you to shine your light and aide me in discovering something beautiful. I wanted to give you my all. I wanted to give you everything you have ever dreamed. Instead you deemed my effort and time unworthy and you felt only pain. At that point, the best way to show you how much I cared and loved you, was to walk away.

Good Enough

Sometimes it is not about being good enough

Sometimes it comes down to one's inability to steer their ship

with you on board.

You

Pain is in your eyes,

Strength is in your smile,

Confidence is in your beauty,

Dreams are in your mind,

Success is in your actions

Gratitude

Time is the most precious jewel that I know. It is sad that not enough people value it. Time brings life, time brings death, time brings hate, and time has brought me to you. For that, time will always have my gratitude

<u>*Trophy*</u>

I should not have to flaunt you like a trophy.

Your worth is way more to me than seeing you as an object.

Negative

Those who negatively oppose your every thought are people that are not meant for your life.

<u>*Lost*</u>

I spent all my time looking for you and when I finally found you I had no idea what to do with you. I was too busy looking for you that I forgot to take the time to look for myself.

Obstacles

When you have a partner that feels like they have to jump through obstacles and walk on eggshells for the people around YOU....how is that fair?

Everyone always will have something to say.
Most of the time their opinions poison the well

I can always be the bad man because I know my heart and I have peace in my mind.

Darkness

Sometimes I need saved from the darkness in my world. The struggle to keep my world bright is a battle that I cannot fully comprehend. Sometimes the darkness consumes everything that I have fought so hard for. On these days I am lost, unable to bring myself back and hate consumes my heart.

Burn

Breaking a man's heart is like spreading napalm. He will scorch everything he touches. Only time can extinguish his flames.

Imperfections

If only you could see what I see

How the beauty of your imperfections

Make you truly perfect.

Personal

When I look right through you, do not take it personally.

No hard feelings from me.

I promise.

No fairytale

Sometimes the things we want most,
we were never supposed to have

Sometimes the people we want most,
we were never supposed to keep.

Learn and keep moving.

A Note to my Younger Self

You will love her more than anything. It is important that you be ready.

Never lose sight of yourself. People will provoke you just for your reaction.

People will hurt you. Learn to forgive and let go. Holding on is poison.

Your success is a result of your determination. Take action and your accomplishments will speak for themselves.

Do not be so hard on yourself. No one is perfect, but always strive for perfection.

Character

I promise you

I will always trust

My character

Over yours

Wildfire

If only you took the time to see that you are the inspiration for the flames in my eyes and in my heart. You are the reason I scorch the earth with every step I take. Without your touch and without your love I am..... Wildfire.

Demons

Sometimes the demons within tug too hard and sometimes it is okay to give up on someone that makes your mind a battlefield.

Translation

Love is often lost in translation

It is not found in all of the obvious places by society's

standards.

Love has remained rooted in the innocence of our children

and the unwavering faith of our elderly.

Be grateful to have love

and cherish every moment it graces your presence.

Bleeding

Sometimes I wonder if you understand how much I bleed for
you.

The craving to bleed ink all over this page for you

Do you understand that I drain myself writing and

contemplating over how much my heart belongs to you?

How much I long for you.

Secrets

If you tell me you have no secrets,
I will tell you not to lie.

I can tell you
that you think of someone
on a lonely night.

You dream how it could be
Or what it would have been.

I am not fooled because there are times
when I cannot erase the thought of you
from my mind.

And then there are times
when I just sit and hold you in my smile.

Words

Sometimes I do not think you understand how much your words fuck with me. My tortured soul will not allow me to stop craving you.

Those Eyes

It's not that I don't like them.

It just scares me

how you wrap me up in them.

The Greatest

Falling for you was one the greatest parts of my life.....in the beginning.

<u>*Anywhere*</u>

Sometimes it is the burning within that is unexplainable.
It is the time I do not want to be anywhere at all but in yours
arms.

Cupid

I am tired of Cupid shooting arrows.

Love that barely sticks.

He needs to evolve into a savage.

I want him to reach inside me

And carve your existence on my bones

And then maybe you will stay.

Superhero

There are mornings when I wake up
And I feel unbreakable like superman

Then there are mornings when I wake up
And I feel alone in a dark place like Batman.

There are mornings when I am motivated
And move as fast as The Flash.

Then there are mornings when I wake up
And I am consumed with rage like the Hulk

Then I realize that all superheroes need saving
And that is when I turn to you.

Dance

When you find a love in someone that destroys everything you thought you knew about love, don't be a coward. Let go and dance in the flames.

Twisted Comfort

Understand that sometimes we ruin great things

because we fail to let ourselves be happy.

When we dance with pain and loneliness for so long,

It becomes, in a sick, twisted way,

our comfort.

The End

And in the end it all burns.

Embrace the burn for exactly what it is.

Learn not to control the flames,

But how to dance within them.

6 Years

I wonder if you ever think of me

Because I have thought about you for the past

72 Months

2,190 Days

52,560 Hours

3, 153,000 Minutes

Not that I have been keeping track.

A Haunting

I crave your existence,

I am haunted by your voice and smile

I do not understand how he is so cruel.

Why won't he give me peace?

Time

How do we not see that time is so powerful?

It holds the knowledge of the world in an infinite cycle of day

and night.

Time has the ability to alter your mood

With too little or too much.

Time can be hope

Time can be doubt.

Time has so much power yet

It cannot be corrupted, bought, bargained with, or stolen.

Time takes what it wants, when it wants

And you have no choice but to surrender.

Mutiny

Beware of whom you allow to ride on your journey, because sometimes the closest people lack loyalty and sometimes they lack the ambition and vision to succeed without sinking your ship first.

The Ocean

Don't be so quick to judge
People are more than what meets the eye.

We are kind of like the ocean
Deep and mysterious but always flowing

Very few actually know their true depths.
Just when you think you know everything
Something else is discovered.

Thoughts and memories
Collide like ships and waves.

Anger is our storm
Calm is our sunshine.

We judge with a narrow mind
And eyes closed.

We all face the same waves and storms
Just at different times and in different forms.